W.H.Wax Publishing Presents

My "Bonus" MOM

Written by **Felicia Graves**

Illustrated by **Jairalin Repalbor**

Written by Felicia Graves
Illustrated by Jairalin Repalbor

Published by
W.H.Wax Publishing, LLC
whwaxpublishing.com

© 2024 Felicia Graves
feliciagravesbooks.com
Illustrations © 2024 Jairalin Repalbor
@bunbunillus_art

Library of Congress Control Number: 2024944516

ISBN: 9781662955129

Proudly Printed in the United States of America

To my bonus daughter, Alanii, who gave me my first chance at motherhood. Coming into each other's lives was a huge adjustment for both of us.

I am truly grateful and honored that God allowed me to parent along with your loving mom and dad.

Our relationship has inspired me to spread positivity and love to other blended families across the world. Continue to be the great, warm-spirited person that you are.

Love you always,
Fe

This book belongs to:

_____

Today is the day
my dad said,

"I do."

Now I have a bonus mom, a mom I can love too.

Just like my mom,
I am loved by each.

She is there at birthday parties, holidays,

and soccer games.

Even at school,
I see her there.

Sitting next to my
mom and dad,
they all love and care.

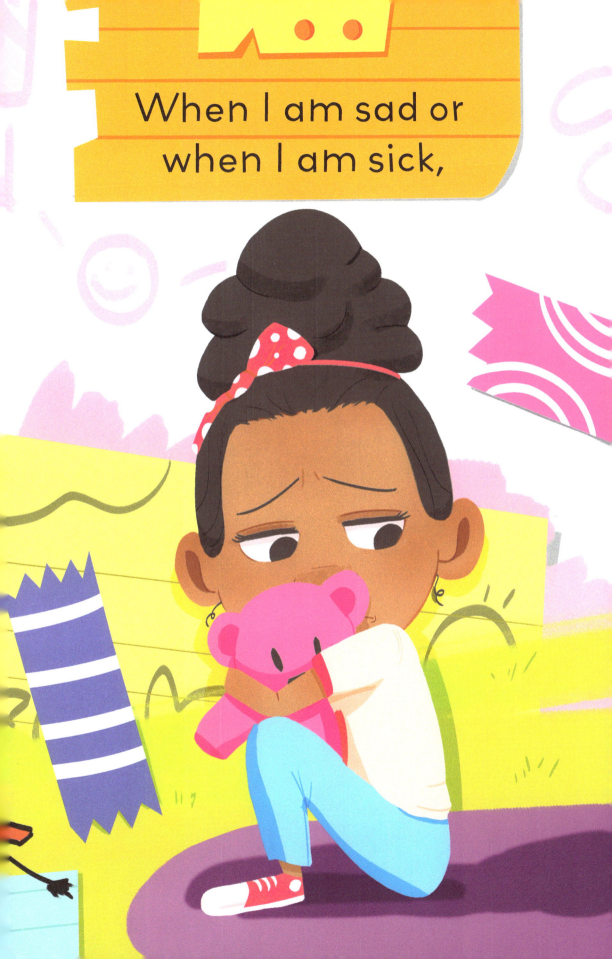

my bonus mom takes
care of me.

She always
knows the trick.

She makes
sure I brush
my teeth and

makes me
bubble baths.

Even when I am wrong, she helps me get on the right path.

We watch movies,
read stories,
and ride bikes.

My bonus mom even kisses
and tucks me in at night.

Just like my mom,
she helps me pray.

I even get to make an extra gift — two on Mother's Day.

If I can't do it and I always feel wrong, my bonus mom lifts me up and tells me to be strong.

how much I love her
with a big hug to show.

When I am away,
I still hear my bonus mom say,

"Good morning, Sunshine!"
and "Have a great day."

Yes, it is true
you can be loved by two.

Oh, how I love
my bonus mom. Yes, I do!

my Dad

Me

my Bonus Mom

About the Author

Felicia Graves is a first-time children's book author who currently resides in South Chesterfield, Virginia.

Growing up in the town of Wytheville, Virginia, Felicia attended college not too far from home at King University where she majored in neuroscience and then extended her education by obtaining her master's in business administration. Following college, Felicia started her career in Medicaid Managed Care, where she has served in various leadership roles over the past 11 years to assist the Medicaid population.

In her spare time, Felicia enjoys traveling the world with her husband and friends. She loves to learn about new cultures and experience the beauty of God's creations. Felicia also spends time playing sports and power lifting with her gym family

About the Illustrator

Jairalin Repalbor aka Bunbunillus lives in the Philippines and is a Freelance Illustrator who loves to work on Picture Books and Cartoon illustrations.

A passionate and skilled illustrator, she worked on several children's books, Mermaid's Don't Wear Floaties, B.e.e Smart, and much more.

Jairalin's goal is to help the younger generation maintain interest in reading illustrative books. Through vibrant visual stimuli and good use of structure and color, Jairalin can help you achieve your goals and bring your ideas to life!

Instagram: @bunbunillus_art

Printed in the USA
CPSIA information can be obtained
at www.ICGtesting.com
LVHW060903091024
792992LV00007B/253

—